# SMART WORDS™
## READER

# COLOSSAL
# CREATURES

Vicky Willows

SCHOLASTIC INC.

# What are SMART WORDS?

Smart Words are frequently used words that are critical to understanding concepts taught in the classroom. The more Smart Words a child knows, the more easily he or she will grasp important curriculum concepts. Smart Words Readers introduce these key words in a fun and motivational format while developing important literacy skills. Each new word is highlighted, defined in context, and reviewed. Engaging activities at the end of each chapter allow readers to practice the words they have learned.

ISBN 978-0-545-93905-8

Copyright © 2016 by Scholastic Inc.

Photos ©: cover: Guenter Guni/iStockphoto; 1: Tim Graham/Getty Images; 2-3: David Fleetham/Alamy; 4: Catmando/Shutterstock, Inc.; 5 background: mihtiander/iStockphoto; 5 inset: NMFS/NOAA; 6-7 background: Hiroya Minakuchi/Minden Pictures; 7 inset: SCIEPRO/Getty Images; 8-9 background: Untrodden Path/Alamy; 8 inset bottom: nelya43/Shutterstock, Inc.; 10 bottom: Paul Fleet/Shutterstock, Inc; 11 top: Hideyuki Utsunomiya/SeaPics.com; 11 inset: Krzysztof Odziomek/Shutterstock, Inc.; 12 soil and sand texture and textures throughout: CG Textures; 12 bottom: kaschibo/Shutterstock, Inc.; 13: Flip Nicklin/Minden Pictures; 14-15: PHOTOCREO Michal Bednarek/Shutterstock, Inc.; 14 inset: David Noton/Alamy; 15 inset: Graeme Shannon/Shutterstock, Inc.; 16-17 background: A & J Visage/Alamy; 16 inset: Scott Buckel/Alamy; 17: A & J Visage/Alamy; 18-19 background: EcoPrint/Shutterstock/Shutterstock, Inc.; 18 inset: Martin Kucera/Shutterstock, Inc.; 19 inset: Albie Venter/Shutterstock, Inc.; 20: Andrzej Kubik/Shutterstock, Inc.; 21: Aleksandar Todorovic/Shutterstock, Inc.; 22-23 background: Sergei25/Shutterstock, Inc.; 22 inset: Cylonphoto/Shutterstock, Inc.; 23 inset: Aleksandar Mitrovic/Alamy; 24 background: Len Jellicoe/iStockphoto; 24 inset: George Lamson/Shutterstock, Inc.; 25 bottom inset: Rebecca E Marvil/Getty Images; 26-27 background: Liz Bradford; 27 inset: Liz Bradford; 28 bottom: Nicola Stratford/iStockphoto; 29: Michael Rosskothen/Shutterstock, Inc.; 30-31: christophe_cerisier/iStockphoto.

10 9 8 7 6 5 4 3                    16 17 18 19 20

Printed in the U.S.A.                    40
First printing, September 2016

Designed by Marissa Asuncion

# Table of Contents

# Chapter 1

# Incredible Titans of the Sea

Earth has an amazing variety of creatures. There are plenty of ways to group animals, including the tallest, shortest, longest, smallest, and most HUMONGOUS.

But where would you find the world's largest animals? Under the sea! A great question to ask is, "Why is this so?"

sperm whales

To find the answer, you need to understand **gravity**. Gravity is the force of attraction that pulls all objects toward Earth. The heavier the object is, the greater the pull of gravity.

The largest animal in the sea today is bigger than a brontosaurus! Structures that support body weight, like muscles and bones, would not be able to sustain such tremendous size on land, and movement would be nearly impossible.

However, in the ocean, there is an upward force, called **buoyancy**. This is the upward push of a fluid on an object. As gravity pulls giant sea creatures down, the pressure of the water beneath them pushes upward, providing an effect of

the North Pacific right whale is the second-largest animal on Earth

weightlessness. This allows the largest creatures to glide gracefully and speedily through the water.

## SMART WORDS

**gravity** the force of attraction that pulls all objects toward Earth

**buoyancy** the upward push of a fluid on an object

# Blue Whale
## Largest Animal on Earth

The blue whale is not only the largest animal on Earth today—it's also the largest animal recorded in Earth's history. The record weight for a blue whale is 380,000 pounds (172,000 kilograms). That's about the same as 2,000 men!

Although whales swim in the seas, they are not fish. Whales are mammals, like you. A mammal is an animal that warms itself internally, has a backbone, has fur or hair, and feeds its babies milk. Whales have fine hairs covering their bodies—they're just hard to see.

blue whale

# Blue Whale: Things That Make You Say WOW!

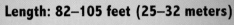

**Length:** 82–105 feet (25–32 meters)

**Weight:** 200,000–300,000 pounds (90,000–130,000 kilograms)

**Size of heart:** 1,000 pounds (450 kilograms)

**Size of tongue:** 6,000 pounds (2,670 kilograms)

## SMART WORD

**mammal** an animal that warms itself internally, has a backbone, has fur or hair, and feeds its babies milk

# Lion's Mane Jellyfish
## Longest Animal on Earth

It's hard to imagine something longer than a blue whale. However, the top spot for the longest animal on Earth is the lion's mane jellyfish. The longest lion's mane jellyfish on record measured 120 feet (36 meters). This record holder comes with a sting!

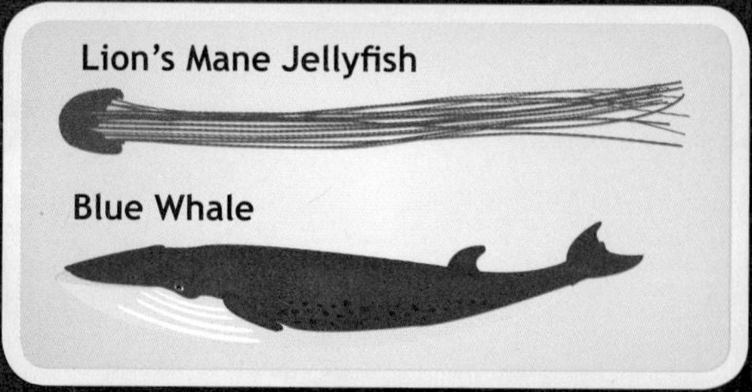

Lion's Mane Jellyfish

Blue Whale

Jellyfish belong to a group of animals called cnidarians [nahy-dair-ee-uh-ns]. The word *cnidarian* means "stinging creature." All cnidarians have circular bodies with long tentacles arranged around their mouths.

lion's mane jellyfish

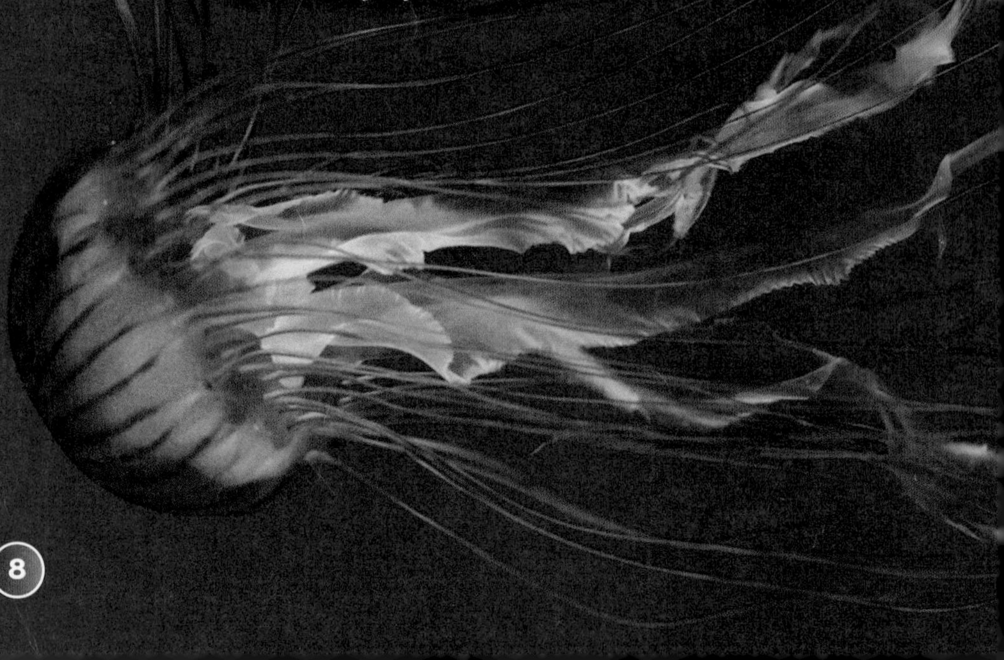

You don't want to meet a lion's mane jellyfish when out for a swim. It has up to 1,200 tentacles, each with stinging cells. These stingers shoot out like tiny harpoons filled with toxin. A toxin is a harmful substance that is produced within living things. The toxin can paralyze prey, making an unsuspecting passerby an easy target for the jellyfish.

Sometimes, the remains of a dead lion's mane jellyfish will wash up on a beach. Be careful near the water when this happens. The stinging cells break off and can survive in seawater for a while— stinging even after the jellyfish dies!

## SMART WORDS

**cnidarian** an animal with a circular body and stinging tentacles arranged around its mouth

**toxin** a harmful substance that is produced within a living thing

# Living Legends

While the blue whale is the largest animal on Earth, the colossal squid is the largest cephalopod in the ocean. You might think of them as the "brainy bunch," as they are very intelligent. Cephalopods are ocean animals with prominent heads, long tentacles, and large eyes. Squids, octopuses, and cuttlefish are all cephalopods. The largest colossal squid ever recorded weighed 1,091 pounds (495 kilograms).

Scientists did not know much about colossal squids for a very long time. These animals are rarely seen, as they live in the deep sea. Early evidence showed up in a surprising place—inside the stomachs of whales. Scientists used the undigested body parts to estimate the size of the squid. For the first time, in 2007, a colossal squid was actually caught on a strong fishing line.

the colossal squid has eyes the size of soccer balls

oarfish

# Biggest Fish

The oarfish is the world's largest bony fish. A fish is an animal that lives in the water, has a backbone, and breathes using gills. Some fish have scales. There are plenty of large fish in the sea, but no other fish reaches the stunning lengths of the oarfish. Oarfish have measured up to 56 feet (17 meters) long and weighed up to 600 pounds (270 kilograms).

The world's largest non-bony fish is the whale shark. These massive fish can grow over 40 feet (10 meters) long and weigh over 40,000 pounds (18,144 kilograms). They have skeletons made up of cartilage, a dense, flexible tissue that is the same material found in the bridge of your nose and outer ear.

whale shark

## SMART WORDS

**cephalopod** an ocean animal with a prominent head, long tentacles, and large eyes

**fish** an animal that lives in the water, has a backbone, and breathes using gills; some fish have scales

**cartilage** dense, flexible tissue that is the same material found in the bridge of your nose and outer ear

11

# Use your SMART WORDS

Match each description with the correct Smart Word.

gravity    buoyancy    toxin    mammal

cnidarian    cartilage    fish    cephalopod

1. This is a harmful substance that is produced by living things.

2. This type of animal has a prominent head, long tentacles, and large eyes.

3. This type of animal lives in the water, has a backbone, and breathes with gills.

4. This is the force of attraction that pulls all objects toward Earth.

5. This is dense, flexible tissue that is the same material found in the bridge of your nose and outer ear.

6. These animals have circular bodies and stinging tentacles that you must watch out for!

7. This force helps you float, as it gives you upward push when in water.

8. This living thing can warm itself from within, has a backbone, has fur or hair, and feeds its babies milk.

Answers on page 32

## Talk Like a Scientist

Use your Smart Words to explain why the world's biggest animals are found in the sea.

# SMART FACTS

## Did You Know?

Whales give birth to live babies. A blue whale baby can drink up to 160 gallons (600 liters) of milk a day and gain about 200 pounds (90 kilograms) a day!

## That's Amazing!

Japanese folklore says that oarfish can help predict earthquakes. As Earth starts to tremble, the fish make rare appearances on the surface of the water.

## Record Breaker!

The world's biggest octopus is the giant Pacific octopus, which can grow to 30 feet (9 meters) and weigh in at 600 pounds (270 kilograms).

# Chapter 2

# Mammoth Land Animals

To find the biggest land animal on Earth today, you will have to travel to Africa. This is where you will find the African elephant, weighing in at 14,000 pounds (6,350 kilograms). This makes it rather small compared to the blue whale, but the elephant must support its own weight on land.

The elephant's natural environment, or **habitat**, is the African grasslands. Here, elephants forage for vegetation for 12–18 hours per day. Each elephant can eat between 200–600 pounds (90–270 kilograms) of leaves, bark, twigs, and branches every day.

## African Elephant: Things That Make You Say WOW!

**Weight:** 4,850–14,000 pounds (2,200–6,350 kilograms)

**Height:** 8–13 feet (2.5–4 meters)

**Size of heart:** 27–46 pounds (12–21 kilograms)

**Heaviest recorded tusks:** 461 pounds (209 kilograms)

**Average life-span:** females–65 years, males–60 years

African elephants travel in **herds** of about 20 to 100. A herd is a large group of hoofed animals that live, feed, and travel together. This offers many advantages, such as protection from predators and sharing in the care of young.

Tusk

african elephant herd

Sadly, the African elephant is in danger of completely disappearing from Earth. The elephant's **tusks**, or its long, pointed teeth, are made of a material called ivory. Elephants are often hunted for their tusks.

## SMART WORDS

**habitat** the natural environment of a living thing

**herd** a large group of hoofed animals that live, feed, and travel together

**tusk** a long, pointed tooth found on animals such as the elephant or walrus

# Reticulated Python
## Longest Snake on Earth

Suppose you were making a scary movie about the world's longest snake. What snake would be the star of your movie? An anaconda? King cobra? The record for the world's longest snake actually belongs to the reticulated python.

A reticulated python is a **reptile**. Reptiles are animals with dry, scaly skin that lay soft-shelled eggs. They are also **cold-blooded**, meaning they cannot warm their own bodies from the inside. Because of this, they are often seen warming themselves in the sun. Other reptiles include turtles, lizards, and crocodiles.

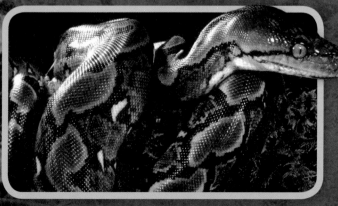

reticulated python

a reticulated python getting a ride in Indonesia

Reticulated pythons are found in Southeast Asia, where they live in moist tropical rain forests. Here, their diamond-patterned backs can be seen slithering through trees and brush. Their favorite prey includes birds, porcupines, monkeys, and other small mammals.

Using 100 curved teeth, the reticulated python firmly takes hold of its prey. The python then wraps its long body around the animal and squeezes tightly. Within a few minutes, the animal is dead and the python swallows it whole.

## SMART WORDS

**reptile** a cold-blooded animal with dry, scaly skin that lays soft-shelled eggs

**cold-blooded** an animal that cannot warm its own body from the inside

# Extreme Heights

Without a doubt, the world's tallest animal is the giraffe. The average male giraffe can grow to 18 feet (5.5 meters) tall. That's about three professional basketball players standing on one another's shoulders! At birth, giraffe babies are taller than most adult humans at 6 feet (2 meters) high.

Groups of giraffes are called towers. Each tower may consist of 12–15 giraffes that spend their days grazing on Africa's grassy plains. Giraffes power-nap, sleeping only 20 minutes per day.

## Giraffes: Things That Make You Say WOW!

**Length of neck:** 6 feet (2 meters)

**Weight of neck:** 600 pounds (270 kilograms)

**Length of legs:** 6 feet (2 meters)

**Length of tongue:** 21 inches (53 centimeters)

**Size of heart:** 25 pounds (11 kilograms)

Like elephants, giraffes are **herbivores.** This means that they only eat plant material. As a group, giraffes are a pretty peaceful bunch as they nibble on treetops. They have very few predators, and can easily escape using their long legs to get away.

giraffe drinking water

Giraffes are in the most danger when they drink water. To reach its tall body all the way down to a watering hole, a giraffe must awkwardly spread its legs and bend its neck. In this lowered position, a giraffe can be an easy target for a hungry lion or crocodile. Good thing for the giraffe that it only has to drink water once every few days!

## SMART WORD

**herbivore** an animal that eats only plant material

# Use your SMART WORDS

Match each description with the correct Smart Word.

> **herd**    reptile    **tusk**
>
> herbivore    **habitat**    cold-blooded

1. I am an animal that eats only plants.

2. I am a long, pointed tooth. On elephants, I am made of ivory.

3. I am an animal that cannot warm myself from the inside.

4. I am a group of hoofed animals that live together, feed together, and travel together.

5. I am a cold-blooded animal that has dry, scaly skin and lays soft-shelled eggs.

6. I am the natural environment of any animal, plant, or other living thing.

Answers on page 32

# Talk Like a Scientist

Use your Smart Words to discuss your favorite animal and its habitat.

# SMART FACTS

## Did You Know?

Giraffes have a small hump on their back like a camel. They also have a spotted pattern like a leopard. This led people to once believe that giraffes were a combination of a camel and a leopard. The early name of a giraffe was "camel-leopard."

## That's Amazing!

African elephants have the largest brain of any land animal. Their brains weigh about 11 pounds (5 kilograms). Elephants display many intelligent behaviors, including grief, compassion, and communication. They can even make music and art!

## Record Breaker!

The largest salamander in the world is the Chinese giant salamander. It grows up to 6 feet (2 meters) and is found in streams and lakes of China. It is endangered, as it is considered a delicacy to eat and is used in Chinese medicine.

# Chapter 3

# Feathered Giants

Up, up, and away! Or not exactly. That's right. The world's largest bird can't get off the ground. This record belongs to the ostrich, weighing 220–350 pounds (100–160 kilograms). Like other birds, the ostrich is **warm-blooded**. This means that they can make their own body heat even when it's cold outside.

Also like other birds, ostriches have feathers and wings. However, the **wingspan** of an ostrich is very small compared to its body. *Wingspan* is the distance across the outstretched wings of a bird from tip to tip. Ostriches primarily use their wings and feathers to attract mates.

## Ostrich: Things That Make You Say WOW!

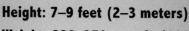

**Height:** 7–9 feet (2–3 meters)

**Weight:** 220–350 pounds (100–160 kilograms)

**Wingspan:** 6.6 feet (2 meters)

**Length of stride:** 10–16 feet (3–5 meters)

**Speed:** Sprint at 43 mph (70 kph)

**Size compared to 6-foot human:**

Ostriches and other modern-day birds do not hold the record for biggest bird ever. Birds known as "terror birds" once roamed the land in South America. Towering up to 10 feet (3 meters) tall and weighing up to 330 pounds (150 kilograms), terror birds were also very speedy. Prey didn't have much of a chance against the 18-inch-long (46-centimeter-long) curved beaks of these birds. They became **extinct** about 2.5 million years ago. An extinct animal no longer exists on Earth.

fossils of an almost complete skeleton of a terror bird were discovered in Argentina in 2010

ostriches use their long, muscular legs to escape predators

## SMART WORDS

**warm-blooded** capable of making heat inside the body

**wingspan** the distance across the outstretched wings of a bird from tip to tip

**extinct** no longer existing on Earth

# Condor
## Biggest Flying Bird

Imagine looking into the sky and seeing a bird with a giant wingspan gliding in the air. This marvelous bird would most likely be a California condor, the Earth's largest flying bird. With their impressive wingspans, condors are commonly mistaken for small planes.

Like all other birds, the California condor has **feathers**. A feather is any flat structure growing from a bird's skin that is made up of a hollow shaft and barbed vanes on either side. Feathers may seem like simple things, but they are engineering marvels.

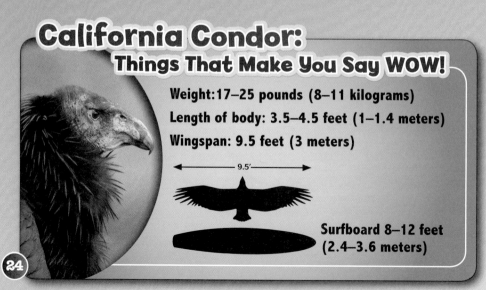

## California Condor:
### Things That Make You Say WOW!

Weight: 17–25 pounds (8–11 kilograms)
Length of body: 3.5–4.5 feet (1–1.4 meters)
Wingspan: 9.5 feet (3 meters)

9.5'

Surfboard 8–12 feet (2.4–3.6 meters)

There are many different types of feathers. Some feathers are specialized for flight. These feathers have vanes that are longer on one side of the shaft than the other. Like an airplane wing, they are designed to take advantage of the buoyant force of air to keep the birds aloft.

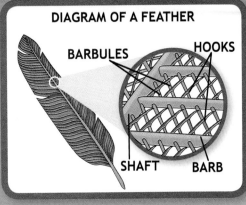

DIAGRAM OF A FEATHER

BARBULES

HOOKS

SHAFT

BARB

You might observe that the condor has no feathers on its head. This is an **adaptation** that helps the birds stay clean. An adaptation is anything that makes an animal better suited for its environment. As **scavengers**, animals that eat the remains of dead animals, condors often have their heads inside a bloody carcass. It pays to have a smooth head!

## SMART WORDS

**feather** a flat structure growing from a bird's skin that is made up of a hollow shaft and barbed vanes on either side

**adaptation** a change that makes an organism or species better suited to its environment

**scavenger** any animal that eats the remains of dead animals

# Prehistoric Giant

In 1983, the remains of a big bird were found outside an airport in South Carolina. This big bird had a wingspan of 21 feet (6.4 meters), as wide as a small plane. The remains belonged to an ancient bird called *Pelagornis sandersi*, the largest known flying bird.

*Pelagornis sandersi* glided over Earth about 25 million years ago. At about 48 pounds (22 kilograms), this bird weighed far less than today's flightless bird, but it was still quite heavy for flight. Scientists think this giant may have just waited for a strong gust of wind to give it lift off the ground.

*Pelagornis sandersi*

Although the California condor is the largest flying bird today, the albatross beats it out for the top spot as far as

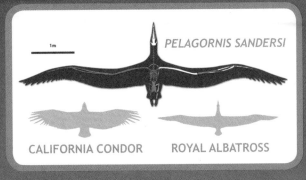

PELAGORNIS SANDERSI

CALIFORNIA CONDOR     ROYAL ALBATROSS

wingspan, with wings stretching up to 11 feet (3.4 meters). Still, neither of these modern-day fliers compare to *Pelagornis sandersi*.

# Use your SMART WORDS

Match each description with the correct Smart Word.

| | | |
|---|---|---|
| **feather** | **extinct** | **warm-blooded** |
| **adaptation** | **wingspan** | **scavenger** |

1. an animal that can generate its own body heat from the inside
2. an animal that eats the remains of dead animals
3. no longer existing on Earth
4. the distance across the outstretched wings of a bird from tip to tip
5. a change that makes an organism or species better suited to its environment
6. a flat structure growing from a bird's skin that is made up of a hollow shaft and barbed vanes on either side

Answers on page 32

# Talk Like a Scientist

Use your Smart Words to talk about your favorite big bird.

# SMART FACTS

## Did You Know?

The California condor was featured on the 2005 state quarter of California. This remarkable bird rebounded from near extinction when, in 1987, only 22 birds existed.

## That's Amazing!

If you are making omelets or baking a cake, it's good to know that one ostrich egg is equal to two dozen chicken eggs. Just in case you're cooking at the ostrich farm!

## Good to Know

The ancestors of birds are actually meat-eating dinosaurs called theropods. This dinosaur group includes the *Velociraptor*, featured in the Jurassic Park movies.

# Glossary

**adaptation:** a change that makes an organism or species better suited to its environment

**buoyancy:** the upward push of a fluid on an object

**cartilage:** dense, flexible tissue that is the same material found in the bridge of your nose and outer ear

**cephalopod:** an ocean animal with a prominent head, long tentacles, and large eyes

**cnidarian:** an animal with a circular body and stinging tentacles arranged around its mouth

**cold-blooded:** an animal that cannot warm its own body from the inside

**extinct:** no longer existing on Earth

**feather:** a flat structure growing from a bird's skin that is made up of a hollow shaft and barbed vanes on either side

**fish:** an animal that lives in the water, has a backbone, and breathes using gills; some fish have scales

**gravity:** the force of attraction that pulls all objects toward Earth

**habitat:** the natural environment of a living thing

**herbivore:** an animal that eats only plant material

**herd:** a large group of hoofed animals that live, feed, and travel together

**mammal:** an animal that warms itself internally, has a backbone, has fur or hair, and feeds its babies milk

**reptile:** a cold-blooded animal with dry, scaly skin that lays soft-shelled eggs

**scavenger:** any animal that eats the remains of dead animals

**toxin:** a harmful substance that is produced within a living thing

**tusk:** a long, pointed tooth found on animals such as the elephant or walrus

**warm-blooded:** capable of making heat inside the body

**wingspan:** the distance across the outstretched wings of a bird from tip to tip

# Index

# SMART WORDS Answer Key

**Page 12**
1. toxin 2. cephalopod 3. fish 4. gravity 5. cartilage 6. cnidarian
7. buoyancy 8. mammal

**Page 20**
1. herbivore 2. tusk 3. cold-blooded 4. herd 5. reptile 6. habitat

**Page 28**
1. warm-blooded 2. scavenger 3. extinct 4. wingspan
5. adaptation 6. feather